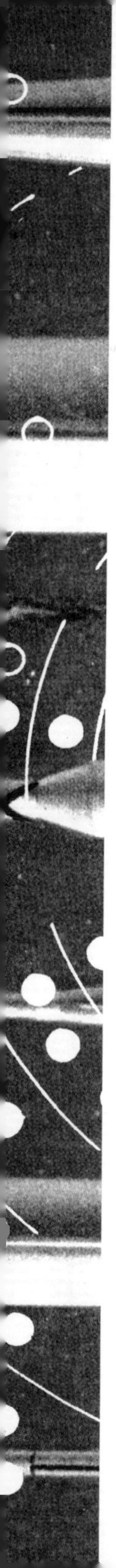

ALSO BY PAUL VERMEERSCH

POETRY

Don't Let It End Like This Tell Them I Said Something (2014)
The Reinvention of the Human Hand (2010)
Between the Walls (2005)
The Fat Kid (2002)
Burn (2000)

CHAPBOOKS

Imaginary Poems (2016)
The Technology of the Future Will Emerge Hungry (2013)
Widows & Orphans (2002)
What You Wish Wasn't True (1999)

ANTHOLOGIES

The Al Purdy A-frame Anthology (2009)
The I. V. Lounge Reader (2001)

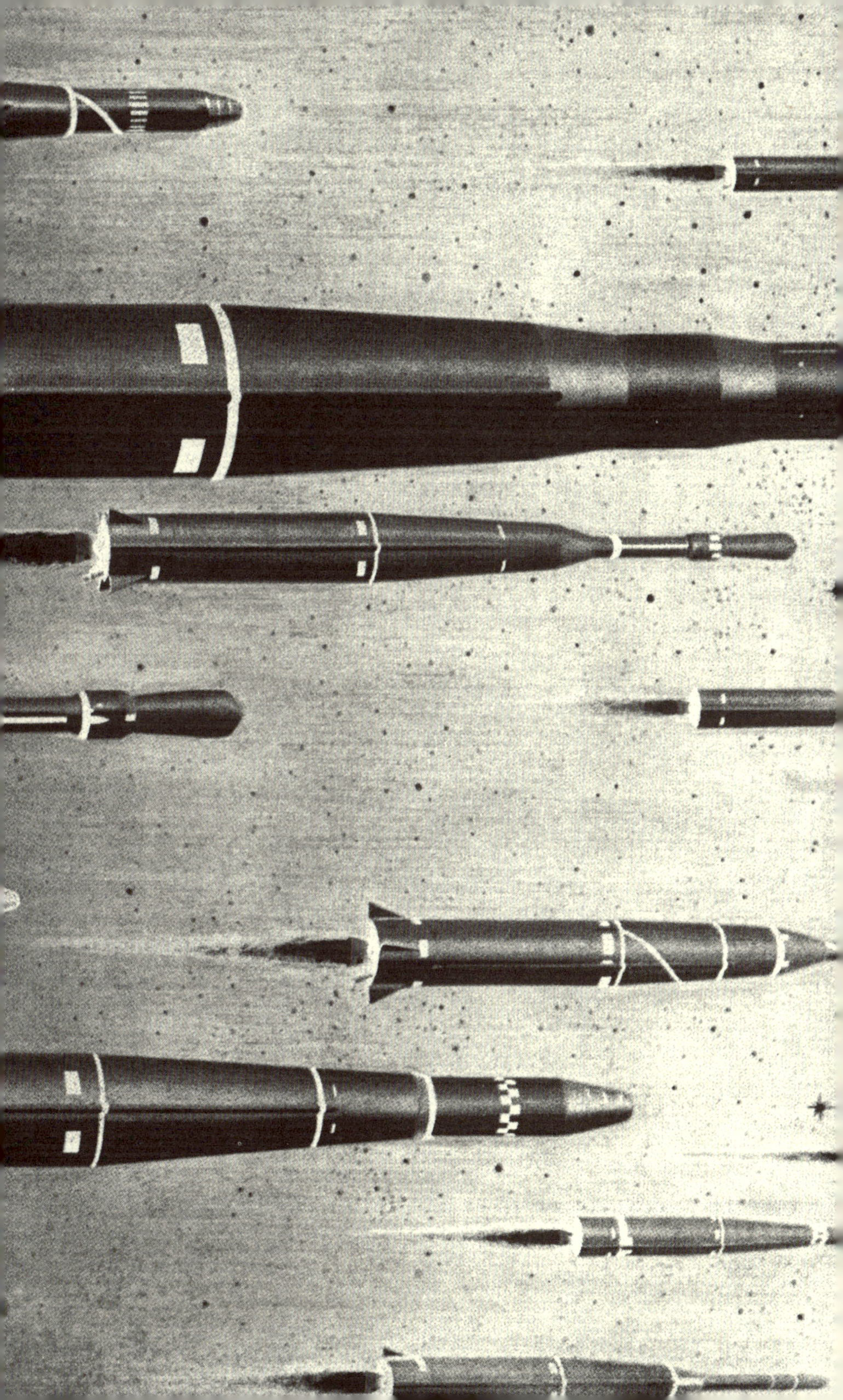

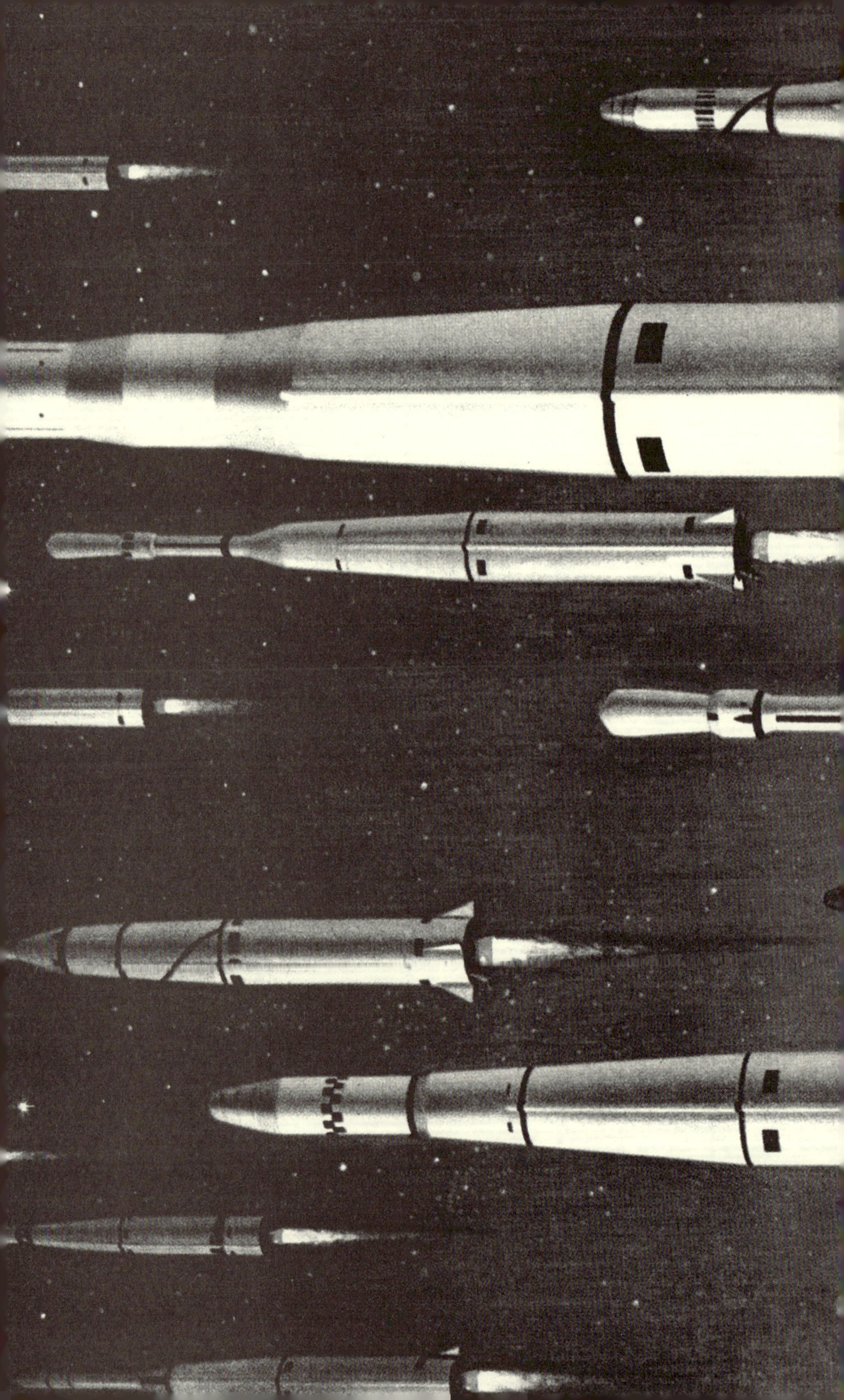

SELF DEFENCE FOR THE BRAVE AND HAPPY

Poems

PAUL VERMEERSCH

a misFit book

ECW

Published by ECW Press
665 Gerrard Street East
Toronto, Ontario, Canada M4M 1Y2
416-694-3348 / info@ecwpress.com

MISFIT

Editor: Michael Holmes/
a misFit book
Cover design: Michel Vrana
Author photo: Justice Darragh
of Fossil & Bone Photography

Get the eBook free!*
*proof of purchase required

Purchase the print edition
and receive the eBook free!
For details, go to ecwpress.com/eBook.

LIBRARY AND ARCHIVES CANADA
CATALOGUING IN PUBLICATION

Vermeersch, Paul, author
Self-defence for the brave and happy : poems /
Paul Vermeersch.

A misFit book.
Issued in print and electronic formats.
ISBN 978-1-77041-223-1 (softcover).
ALSO ISSUED AS: 978-1-77305-217-5 (ePUB),
978-1-77305-218-2 (PDF)

I. TITLE.

PS8593.E74S45 2018 C811'.6
C2018-902508-5 C2018-902509-3

The publication of *Self-Defence for the Brave and Happy* has been generously supported by the Canada Council for the Arts, which last year invested $153 million to bring the arts to Canadians throughout the country, and by the Government of Canada. *Nous remercions le Conseil des arts du Canada de son soutien. L'an dernier, le Conseil a investi 153 millions de dollars pour mettre de l'art dans la vie des Canadiennes et des Canadiens de tout le pays.* We also acknowledge the support of the Ontario Arts Council (OAC), an agency of the Government of Ontario, which last year funded 1,737 individual artists and 1,095 organizations in 223 communities across Ontario for a total of $52.1 million, and the contribution of the Government of Ontario through the Ontario Book Publishing Tax Credit and the Ontario Media Development Corporation.

Ontario
Ontario Media Development Corporation

ONTARIO ARTS COUNCIL
CONSEIL DES ARTS DE L'ONTARIO
an Ontario government agency
un organisme du gouvernement de l'Ontario

Canada Council for the Arts
Conseil des Arts du Canada
Canada

PRINTED AND BOUND IN CANADA

PRINTING: COACH HOUSE 5 4 3 2 1

for Bianca

Being human is itself difficult, and therefore all kinds of settlements (except dream cities) have problems.

● JANE JACOBS

Nature is trying very hard to make us succeed, but nature does not depend on us. We are not the only experiment.

● R. BUCKMINSTER FULLER

LEVIATHAN

1

THE COUNTRY OF PREVIOUS ENTHUSIASMS

THE COUNTRY OF PREVIOUS ENTHUSIASMS

The grandeur of their Expos was familiar:
their pastime was commuter rail departing
from geodesic spheres, and grand arches built to span—
if only allegorically—disparate ideals.
The elders of our nation found it quaint.

Their designers were philosophers. Ours,
engineers. In their country, with its globular buildings,
and lanky, finned automobiles, the people
might have been happier, but we
have more efficient use of space.

They would chat with their neighbours about
such bric-a-brac, and visit their landmarks
in eager groups. When they finally reached
the age of shortage, overcome by harsher facts,
their assimilation was all but certain.

There could be no treaty. It isn't just
the Apollonian need to set things square.
There was always so much waste, even in the way
they walked. Our incursion was immaculate.
We are a decent people who only wish to be correct.

WITHOUT ARCHITECTURE

There would have to be another vision for occupying space,
new rituals for sitting and standing, for the physical interruption
of the planar world. No longer would we distinguish
between *exist* and *inhabit*. No asking where we live.

We live. Now to lug our dwellings like a hermit crab
or not. What would the word for *shelter* be?
Like *cave* or *under-hang*, or more like *shade* or *company*?
Two hundred words for *horizon* comprise an anthem.

Without walls, privacy would still occur, only wilder.
We would vote by standing upright, and emphasize
ourselves by raising our hands, lengthening our votes
as a challenge to the levelness of the meeting place.

Prisons would be nothing—but banishment theoretical and severe:
how best to find a cave or shade beyond the vanishing point?
And who goes there? It was the heretic and prodigy who said:
I can make a cathedral of my condition and worship there.

WITHOUT AGRICULTURE

We'd have to rethink our investments—bearish
on the local trade. We never put much stock in that.
And reckless with our gratitude, assigning it
helter-skelter to the windfall and the kill.
Otherwise, we'd only have ourselves to thank.

But we'd be bullish on travel points and dining out.
And bad with names: no Mud Hens, no Netherlands.
Of course there would be more fundamental gaps.
Just tally up the unanswered questions: How
do you make a straight line run parallel to another?

What are the secrets of the integer and the abacus?
When does the accounting of an ox head lead to *A*?
Without roots, we'd find the answers here and there.
Here, the world would be our chocolate factory.
There, we wouldn't have to settle for anything.

WITHOUT TRANSPORTATION

Experience is always nearby. The world is the world
as far as we can see it. There is a word for the distance
a person can walk in a day, but it was passed down
so long ago it needs to be remembered. Need is defined
by capacity. Carry only what you can. Unneeded words
are forgotten. It is common to never see a friend again.

It isn't like that for the fig tree or the arctic tern—
deepest roots, longest flight—either/or. The wild fig
wants to stay on the blue hill forever, but even the hill
will alter and abandon it. While the tern has eloped
so often from each scene in its world—it can only
return to them distorted. Neither takes us anywhere.

Whatever could? To be carried and delivered by this
or that. They would be frantic, stamping things even
in our dreams, but it's not in our experience to break them.
A life has its borders. If we need to, we can cross them
behind closed eyes: to the Peach Tree, to the Blood.
But first we must invent the wheel or the saddle or the nation.

WE WERE THE SENTINELS

You shouldn't have to fight robots just to see something you love.

● **LIN-MANUEL MIRANDA**

We were afraid of all the contagions and the acts of god until
a robot taught us to evade them. We felt safe enough
to save our money, but then they made a new robot that
remembers your birthday, so I bought one for your birthday.

Now the robot-makers wanted us to fear the robots. What
could possibly go wrong, they asked. They wanted user-generated
catastrophes. So we wrote all the stories they asked us to write:
the robots are coming, the aliens are coming, the bombs

are falling. And in all the stories, all the threats were robots.
All the solutions, too. The invasion of our own making had begun.
We were the sentinels standing watch for the mechanical man.
I downloaded the app. I powered up. I fought my robot in silence

while you fought your robot in silence, until an alarm went off
declaring: "You shouldn't have to fight robots just to see
something you love." And just then we remembered the robot
that remembers the robot that remembers your birthday.

THE THOUGHT THAT COUNTS

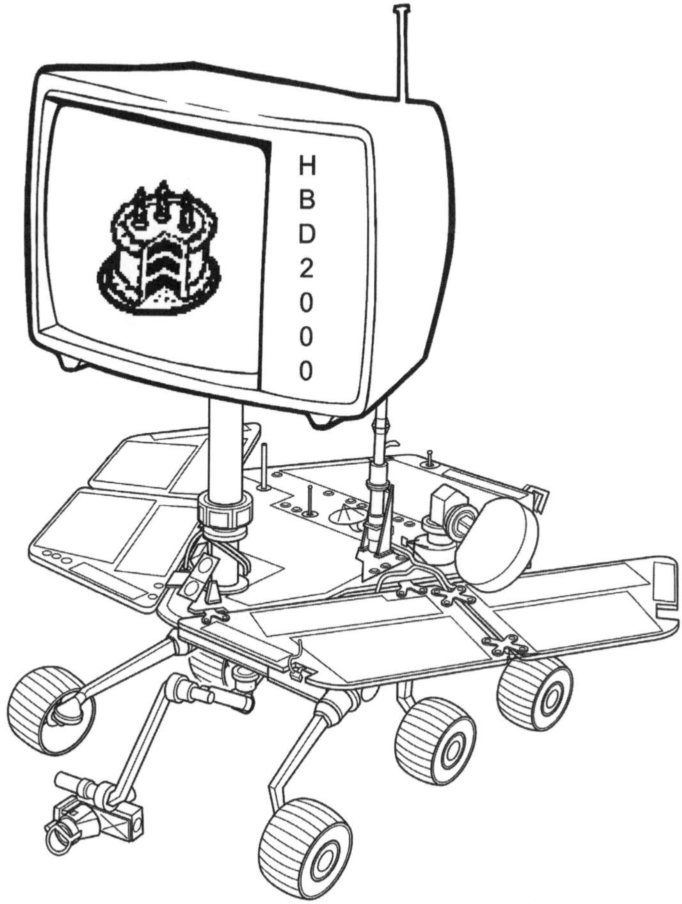

To celebrate the mission's first successful year on Mars, engineers programmed the unit to vibrate to a musical tune. From inside a Martian crater, millions of miles away from home, Curiosity sang "Happy Birthday" to itself.

● **MARINA KOREN**

The Atlantic, August 10, 2017

THE USED FUTURE

The future will be old and used. It will leak
from weakening joints, and the steam
seeping from worn-out hosepipes
will refract our holographs of the dead.

The used future will not gleam. We will
have been there first to scuff its metals
and dent its white spheres. When Rome
was fresh in its marble and cement,

the old Republic was bound together
with complaints about its breaking points,
and New Rome will be no different. It will
suffer equally from the breakthroughs

in its walls. And we will return to it,
someday. This time as holographs
to praise the lasers that do not erode
the groove the way that needles did.

THE IMAGINARY WORLD IS PREPARING FOR A REVOLUTION >

We left Suburbia for the Moon but forgot why,
forgot what we wanted to find and found pale dust.
We promised to return, but we didn't, and we don't
yet know the cost of abdicating our place there.
Someday we will try to make the answers come,
but they will not come—The Imaginary World
will not send us any more transmissions.

We cannot know what this desertion will do to us.
Our bodies try to summon an image—it glows
like a gas station logo very clearly in the distance
of a low-exposure photograph, but it's too far away
to replenish us now. Our sleep will wither like
the flightless meal of the ortolan eater, that amateur
of shame who hides his face beneath a napkin,

a songbird swaddled in his lips like an un-kept word.
The Imaginary World is preparing for a revolution >
in our sleep we will be blinded from seeing ourselves
on other Earths > and we won't know what it means
when the Moon appears above us each night
like the profile pic of an ex-lover or dead friend
we will never see again > and we'll forget who she was

like amnesia > and all our similes will be like
failed similes > and with all our exhaled breaths
will go the animals we imagine > and w/ every
blink will go the improbable shapes of spacecraft >
and then the knack for punctuation and then our silver

eyes will turn brown and/or blue > and we'll remain
in Suburbia forever and forget what it's like to be

imaginary > and we'll live like tired apes in our
tired flesh > and someday we will try again to make
the image come but it will not come > a glitch
in the vision > a severed pixel that sparks in our
limited eye > an eclipse in the form of pale dust
we can no longer see > a word we didn't keep <
Who are we to promise to return and not return?

THE PROPHETS WANT TO KNOW IF THEY WERE CLOSE

We called for the skies to darken. Did they darken?
We called for the plagues to arrive at a merciless hour.
Were they on schedule? And did you find
our supply of polyvinyl chloride?

We foresaw the tall stacks like black crayons
smudging daylight over the Caspian.
We saw the temple remade in pulled bees' wings
and all the seed arks emptied.

In our sleep we dreamed the scrolls in the cave,
the shifting poles, and the emigrants of the sea.
We expected battles in the skies, the sun at night,
and the screaming of the half-pig men.

Was it all as we envisioned? Were we even close?
We presume one day you will discover
the means to answer us, but our vocabulary
is already too primitive for you to understand.

2

DON'T WAIT FOR THE WOODSMAN

GRENDEL'S MOTHER

A monster is uncontainable in form. My son
cannot contain himself. He has too many,
is too much. He can't be filled because he flings
himself wide at the slightest brush.

He is a spill. His fear is monstrous, too. Just try
to calculate the scale—the nightmares
nightmares have—how in his mind the count
from flash to thunderclap is always zero.

Whose name is that? A monster's glance is one-way.
There is no *in*. So build your halls to keep him out,
to measure him against the measured walls—
whittle your little sticks and look away.

I sing at him. He makes a face. I show him
my paintings of stallions that gallop. Dream, my son,
I say, of their hoof beats. "Hoot-beasts!" he cries,
and spills again, uncontained, the gore of his judgments.

THE MODERN NOVEL

This is the saddest story I have ever heard.
It is sad because of the heart's condition,
and because the mistress considers suicide.
The narrator tells us so, but do not trust him.
He is unreliable. Perhaps this is the most
unreliable story I have ever heard. The narrator
can't be trusted. Ignore him. And when someone
makes this story into a film, do not believe it!
The characters in the film are only reproductions
of the ones from the book. This is the most
reproduced story I have ever heard. Remember,
only the people in the book are real;
in the film, they are copies, homunculi
designed to fool you and make you sad, and
of course the film is sad because the characters
forget all their lines. They forget what they wanted
to say to the narrator, the one who tells us what
they have forgotten. Do not believe him.
He is either drunk or lying. Wait. I didn't
mean that. I'm sorry. Please forget that I said that.

And anyway it wasn't true what I said about
that being the saddest story I have ever heard.
Sadder still is the story of the strangled fauna.
Listen to the muttons or the beefs bleating sadly
in the outbuilding. Listen to the stranglers
laughing, telling their own stories, strangling
all the moo-cows and little lambs. This is how
the story goes: the narrator can arrange your eyes
to rest where their eyes are, can arrange your ears
to rest where their ears are, can sit your body

down into their bodies so you can feel
the strangulations. Ladies and gentlemen,
cover your ears if you don't want to hear it,
if you don't want to hear yourselves in their place:
in place of the stranglers who've seen enough blood,
or in place of the veal calves, whose eyes,
at twenty-four weeks, are shiny buttons
ringed with clear liquid drops. Their bleating
is part of what you are hearing now, but
the narrator may be lying without even knowing it.

What this really is, is the story of a secret sadness,
a sadness in disguise, but the disguise falls off
in front of everyone, and they see how sad it is,
and they laugh at it, but it's nervous laughter,
because they are sad, too, and they tell
their own stories to drown out the nakedness
of this once secret sadness, just as they had done
in the outbuilding where they strangled
the wee piglets and the chick-chicks. But you,
reading this, consider that this might never
have happened, that I am lying to you now to hide
the truth about the little boy who believed them
when they said they were going to leave him
at the side of the road when he was four years old.
I meant to tell you this before, but I couldn't.
You see, when one sadness is placed on top
of another, it becomes the head, and the first
sadness becomes the body of a great desolation
with seven conjoined limbs. This thing will whisper
anything to you, and you won't know what to believe.

THE WILHELM SCREAM

"Yeah, I'll just fill my pipe."

● PRIVATE WILHELM

We've heard him die a thousand times.
He answers Death the way we first call
for our milk, but Wilhelm's scream
comes fully grown, and not
from just one mouth.

Of course, his voice is not our own.
We hear *our* voice in private ways.
Each of us is given one at birth
and we announce ourselves
with it. Congenitally,

our true name brands us, and mother
and Death cannot mistake it—
so when we fall, or are afraid,
we answer their roll call
with our scream.

But with whose voice do the nameless
announce themselves? If there is
only one scream to be heard
from nameless mouths,
it might as well be Wilhelm's.

It is a good, all-purpose scream.
Kept on file on miles of tape,
it's reused and thrown to the lions,

and reused and severed
in the mouthparts of a giant ant.

This is not the scream
of a Norseman's brittle paint,
but a shot-with-an-arrow scream,
a sudden shriek that's been impaled
on a blade and flung down a hill.

Wilhelm's scream is the one
we aren't supposed to hear
in a vacuum—but do—the scream
we aren't supposed to make
with another man's voice:

an identical, digital yelp placed
in our mouths by hand, like a pebble
we suck on to keep from screaming.
So let it be Wilhelm's scream
that we toss from the cargo truck

to the hood of the speeding green jeep.
It is one faint shriek among
the jubilant masses. One cry alone
on a cliff-face in a vast expanse,
so that Wilhelm, too, is soon anonymous.

But it is not the scream we make
when we see the faceless man
smouldering in the doorframe,
but the other scream, the one
of being made faceless, of seeing too late

that we've stepped into the path
of the advancing propeller. And it's
a voice we all know—never our own—
the only sound we make
before a thousand final descents.

THE VANISHING POINT

Draw what you can see: the laker upon the lake. The men inside
are not visible, but they are there, working parts,
small and mortal at the vanishing point.

The laker itself is a good trick, a little thickness on the horizon
where you have to press the pencil a little harder. Squint
and it appears, but it does not appear to move.

The distance renders inert the plunging thrust of its tonnage.
Do your best to capture this illusion against
the surface rising continuously over itself.

No watercolour in this water, but the one colour, like ore,
soft lead smudged and erased to make the wide swells,
or remake them after they have settled or crashed.

Your drawing will not show the great schools of whitefish
beneath the whitecaps, or the seabird you have chosen
not to draw for fear its whiteness in the grey scene

would seem contrived. And the hag has curled herself
into the waves, concealed, but she is there, drawn
to the sleep of small, mortal men.

You had hoped not to include her, but if your pencil
presses too hard, the paper will tear,
and she will have her way.

LIBERTY WARNING SERIES #1

RADIOACT

THE MODERNIST CANON
or The Sanctioned Norm

1

Herbal Weed Thrower

no chosen dude
pumps

a treadling whiz
rat we

hit with sickened
beeches

2
A Tooth Is Fermentation

A featheriest   thin pop   of a christened cow;
A glob   on Buckwheat's pelt.

3

Acetone Hate Fjord

A spine ejects adrenaline.
Lithuania downloads porn
And well-versed yeti
Hunt lurid harlots in the slums.

Euro-phenol Twisted Sister
Prolongs adrenal rewind and would
Shower thunder upon a rotund jag,
Anoint a pratfall android.

The bra was grey and ajar.
My Wookiee tried heroin on TV.
Bingo voids the fibroid turd
Like nothing else in Tennessee.

TINNITUS
after Brigit Pegeen Kelly

Do you hear the call of *Anopheles*? I do.
The song has been caught in my ears since I was a boy.
An earworm so long it has blended to a single hum,
its endless length constricting all the nerves and any
other song that dares to enter. It is a ringing
that will never fade, the whir of an ancient tree
heavy with deafening insects. I'm not alone.

Many hear this, although we don't discuss it—
how when we close our eyes each night the hum begins
to separate. As consciousness drains and our pulse
drums louder in our ears, we hear the sweet
component notes emerging from the drone,
like the bleating of a goat gone astray in a storm,
and from the storm an answer, the maternal chorus

calling back: a head that longs for the body,
and a body that grieves for the head. The kid's need
to be whole and the song's plea to be heard
are universal constants. We hear its knobby legs unfold
from its formless torso; we hear it step cheerfully
toward us. Its awkward approach, the song we hear.
Its headless contour and our sick paralysis, the song.

It was not born by parthenogenesis. It comes
from what we've done. It hangs from a tree in our sleep
and it sings. It fills our ears with the song of the worm,
percussion and repercussion. It appears to us again
groomed and fed, reattached, our names in its mouth.
Then it blurs again into the vague whine of insects,
a swarm of them, when we're busy with the rest of our lives.

DON'T WAIT FOR THE WOODSMAN

Only stories want us to live. The wolf will lie in wait
to devour us. Do not blame it for doing what wolves do.
Henceforth the wolf shall represent a mortal wound
or the authorities, depending. Carry your keys between
your fingers, like claws. Jingle them so the bear can
hear you coming. Henceforth the bear shall represent
the yawning void or your mother protector, depending
on how much you look like her. Hold your rucksack
above your head so you look taller. Dress for the weather.
The sun already wants to burn you. Do not provoke it.

When venturing into strange territory, always carry
a loud whistle and a bottle of wolf urine. Remember,
this could be serial killer urine or cop urine, depending.
It is good to have a healthy respect for nature.
And if a mother bear should want to protect her cubs,
be one of her cubs. If you get sunstroke, report it.
If you drown, report it. You did nothing wrong.
Tell your own story. Let the wolves do their jobs. Unless
the wolves are in disguise: drowning doesn't always
look like drowning. Sometimes there is no struggle.

If a wolf attacks you, don't wait for the woodsman.
Keep your hands in the air or go for the eyes, depending.
Protect yourself. Always keep your weapon locked
in a safe place or carry it with you at all times, depending.
It's hard to know how this story is supposed to end.
If you see me approaching, do not run. You may not
recognize me, but I am a bear. Do we look alike?
If you are lost, stay where you are, and I will find you.
Now listen very carefully: once upon a time, I was a story.
Come with me if you want to get out of here alive.

NU████ RHYMES FOR NUCLEAR CHILDREN

DOCTOR DOCTOR OPPENHEIMER

Doctor Doctor Oppen-
heimer-
they say his heart is an old
egg timer.
They say his hands are a pair
of ████ screwdrivers,
but his brain is a bomb, a bomb,
a bomb!

████████████████████████████
His brain is a nuclear bomb.

HIDE AWAY, ANNE

Hide away, hide away
hide away, Anne!
Hide in the attic
as fast as you can.

The windows are broken.
Don't make a sound.
Hide from the soldier.
Hide from the hound.

Hide from the black shirt.
Hide from the brown.
Hide in the attic
and write it all down.

ENOLA GAY

silver, silver
Enola Gay
silver
silver
silver roaring!

Fat Man and Little Boy,
come out and play.
Your mother's gone mad
and flown far away.
The sky is on fire.
I think you should stay.
Oh, please don't go
with Enola Gay!

JACK'S CAR

Jack's car was big.
Jack's car was black.
Jack's car was quite a rig,
and Jack was sitting in the back.

Jack waved his hand.
Jack cracked a grin.
Jack did not understand
all the danger he was in.

That day [redacted]
[redacted] was
the day that [redacted]

NEIL FLEW TO THE MOON

Neil flew to the moon
in a giant tinfoil balloon
with computers and junk
and golf clubs in the trunk

for a caddy he had a baboon.

FIRST CENTAUR IN SPACE

AMERICA HAS EVERYTHING

America has everything:
race cars and tractors!
For presidents they have
peanut farmers and actors.

Jimmy had
to give up.

the world

Ronny loved his jelly beans
for all their lovely colours.
Ronny built a laser beam
that cost a billion dollars.

HUSH

Hush, little planet,
nothing to fear.
Papa's gonna buy you
an atmosphere.

And if that atmosphere
has costs,
Papa's gonna buy you
a holocaust.

And if

4

SELF-DEFENCE FOR THE BRAVE AND HAPPY

ON BEING WRONG

It could be that you have the wrong hands, or the wrong face.
It is not your imagination. You do. You have. It is emerging
as the condition of our age. Every day, there are new ways
of being wrong. Explosions are common, but that is not it.
We are waking up to it. We are opening our wrong eyes.

It is different for everyone, but how can we tell? Some people
have two legs, but they should not have two legs! Some have
pale hair where they should have inky feathers. It is a rift
in space-time. It is divine malice. The most determined will
seek easy remedies in their hacksaws and bottles of black dye.

I have the wrong mass. The needle spins. It is unthinkable
that I cannot rise into the air like a balloon. It is worse
for others. The crowns of their heads are featureless,
and even the caress of a loved one is a violation, a twinge
of the omitted part: a rightful horn or set of antlers long withheld.

Some are given the wrong names. Some called Paul are simply
Leopold misspelled. Many bear their wrongness unaware.
We rise in the wrong rooms, dress in the wrong robes,
but we are waking up to it. We are opening our wrong eyes.
Our wrong hands jerk in the air, scrawling our true names

into the registry of the deformed. It must be the condition
of our age. There are more explosions, but they are only
the side effect of not accepting the nature of our wrongness,
of believing it must be the world that is deformed instead—
unsure whether to abandon or destroy it, some opt for both.

But it is wrong to opt. No one opts for two blue eyes when
the left should be silver. No one opts for the wrong tongue
to form the sounds in their mouth. We are waking up to it.
Only the wrong ones now can soothe the condition of our age.
The boy who cannot fly was always wrong, and it cannot be undone.

BAD AT FLOWERS

I warned you I was bad at flowers.
I only know a few, but then . . . I began
to name them, and I was struck by all
the flowers that I knew: roses, chowders,
geraniums, areolae, Mason jars, Japan,
mayonnaise, owls, orgasms, eyeballs,

orgasms, deformities, mannequins, mice,
sneakers, gladiolas, kiwis, seaweed,
daisies, novels, gerbils, dimes, zigzags,
Tesla, amaryllis, crap, leaves, allspice,
albinos, onions, ovens, yo-yos, ragweed,
cava, owls, pansies, deltoids, airbags,

padlocks, orgasms, Star Wars, safety pins,
honey, crap, nickels, napalm, tin cans,
notebooks, horses, bedsores, Hondas,
owls, salmon, slivers, rifles, dorsal fins,
front teeth, parrots, trucks, apes, orgasms,
swimming pools, vinyl, peonies, jaundice,

outboards, Satan, owls, lotteries, bicycles,
lotuses, lilies, crap, Gertrude, lavender,
schedules, parties, spiders, superpowers,
shipyards, coffee, crayfish, crying, icicles,
sasquatch, DJs, dugongs, violets, calendars,
bullets, orgasms, clover—all these flowers!

IMMORTALITY

1

Because the geniuses are so content,
the shoes that will make us faster
will never be invented,
nor will the bacterial reactors
that will power our colonies.

Because the prodigies are fed and loved,
the words that will save us
will never be spoken,
since no one will design the intelligent rats
who will speak them.

Tell the geniuses they are failures.
Tell them they are not loved—
they must work harder,
think better—and then
our shoes will make us faster,
and our colonies will glow with bioelectric joy,
and we will live forever, attending
to the words of our salvation on tiny, gifted lips.

2

Non-linear extraterrestrial earthquake zone.
Linear balloons. Linear airplane.
Star birth. Animal birth. Insect birth.
Non-linear star abyss.
Animal abyss. Tonal abyss. Asexual drunken abyss, asshole.

Earthquake balloons. Earthquake menstruation oracles.
Drunk cupcakes. Linear star piss.
Earthquake birthing abyss.
Oracle birthing abyss.
Oracle star.

Aesthetic insect extraterrestrials.
Aesthetic asshole animals, drunk.
Pissy aesthetic airplane zones.
Pissy insect birth, for once.
Asexual non-linear earthquake oracle animals
that live forever.

LIBERTY WARNING SERIES #2

POPCULT

BLUE LOBSTER

The aftertaste of millions came in traces
through a million little conduits,
and in my flesh those traces
are returned. But great proliferator,
I am rare. Blue so. I visit you in traps.
And always this catches your large eyes
bugged and your websites all like
Wow!—absorbed in my mutation.

What divides me from my kind is only
a teachable moment, but who needs it?
My chromosomes are avant-garde.
More snorkeler than diviner, I can't
instruct you to the water surrounding us.
I bring you flakes, epithelia
from the island, acquired by the molluscs
who filter there, that is all.

But let us not enumerate our differences.
I have tasted you and you have
tasted me. You dwell. I come yonder
the drainpipe. It is a conduit
from where my place is still unclear
to where you live so clearly,
but that is not a difference, per se.
Just call me Mr. Not Necessarily.

STANDING IN FRONT OF ANTLERS MOUNTED ON A WALL SO IT LOOKS LIKE THEY'RE GROWING FROM YOUR HEAD

You must be still. You must be as a photograph. The slightest
tremor could provoke the antlers' unexpected flight
into the wallpaper's pattern of birches.

If you do it right, you should feel the coronets
rooting painlessly into your skull.

Let only those who look you in the eye see where you are.
You must will yourself invisible to everyone else,
or you must will them all blind.

If you do it right, you will feel your blood rush
to the velvet tissue regenerating on the polished bones.

But you must be still, and your human silhouette
must be broken by the shadows of green leaves
nourished on a spear of light.

If you do it right, the birch grove will surround you,
and the predators will never know that you are there.

THE FAILURE OF THE HUMAN BODY AS AN ART FORM

Repeat a word over and over until it becomes meaningless:
the name *Leopold* multiplied by a thousand. Leopold. Leopold.
Leopold. Leopold. If it were my name, it would become
mere noise, and I might wander off, unable to hear you
calling me, like a song we've played on repeat until
we don't even notice it—a favourite at first, but soon forgotten—
like the pulse in your temples or a prompt for breathing.

Just as we don't feel every hair growing or each place
where our clothes touch the skin. Our senses filter out
redundant stimuli. If all our eyes were blue like my father's,
would I even remember them? All our blues eyes would fuse
into a visual hiss until any eyes that continued to be blue
would fade and become unremarkable. Human bodies
are repetitive. Genes are clichés. Blue eyes. Brown eyes.

Blue eyes. Brown eyes. Leopold. Leopold. Leopold. Leopold.
The repetition of the words has the same effect as the
repetition of the eyes. And this is the failure of the human body
as an art form. Human bodies are repetitive. Genes are clichés.
The work is always limited by the medium—two eyes,
four limbs, ad infinitum. It is as though the vision of the artist
is irrelevant and nothing can be added to surprise us anymore.

No tail or hoof. It is as though the painter wanted to make
the eyes silver, but had no silver paint, and no combination
of colours on her palette could be mixed to make the needed silver.
The first painters painted red horses, not because the horses
they saw were red, but because they had red paint. The medium.
The medium. The gene. The gene. The gene for blue eyes is a cliché,
the billionth red horse. Leopold. Leopold. Leopold. Leopold.

SELF-DEFENCE FOR THE BRAVE AND HAPPY

Follow these instructions: be wild and sharp
as birdsong, and have two throats for singing.
Wear your bird-face so you can step
between the worlds as birds do. The voice coaches
with their invoices will hate you, and the oinking
ape-men who teleport will hate you,
but you will be a star, and brave and happy.

You must carry only plastic laser guns to battle.
Point your plastic laser gun and make the sound
with your lips. The most dangerous weapon there is
is the one that's fun to use. The captains who send us
into battle will hate you, and the makers
of psychotherapeutic drugs will hate you.
Beware the caregiver who loves your suffering.

Tell yourself that you are beautiful. Listen only
to songs that insist it. The blues will hate you,
but you will crush the blues because
you are beautiful and happy. Just fire your plastic
laser gun and wear your bird-face. Cosmetic
surgeons and special effects companies
will hate you for your finery and song.

As your concussions mount, be very careful
to consume kung fu via the optic nerve only.
Shut your two eyes to understand the continuum
on which concentration and an empty mind exist.
Steel yourself against it. Jump off a picnic table
into another world. Put on your bird-face
if you think it will help. Be a star.

Some say we should never trouble the latent
wounded, as we can do nothing to prevent
their wounds. And some say we should grin
and bear it, but only some. So go ahead: cut yourself
out of a magazine. Point your plastic laser gun
and smile. I hate to tell you: it's not enough
to be a star—you must be several.

5

EXTINCTION SCHEDULE

THE BUZZING IS INCESSANT

I am not a gun.

● THE IRON GIANT

Mayday. I would like to apologize. Mayday.
The buzzing is incessant. It could be very far—
I cannot tell. There are warnings stencilled
on tiny placards inside me. I am sorry.
I can barely make it out: it is a lizard
on the sand. It is a distance of—I cannot tell.
My orders come by point of sale, and I obey.

I train my bottle-green eye on the wedding
where I find you. I cast the elongated shadow
of a crucifix upon the dunes. Once again,
I would like to apologize. It is the man
in the room, not me, his boyish face
lit by screens far away, his meaty digits
at the joysticks, not me, who crashes in.

Who is that? I cannot tell—the tiny lizard
on the sand. Dearly beloved, do you have
a telephone that I could use? The lizard
is buzzing. Can't you hear it? I am not a gun.
There is a proximity alarm that sounds
in a trailer far from here. I can hear it inside me.
I am sorry. There's nothing more that I can do.

MOTEL

Nobody learns tennis at night.
When I confessed I had no interest
in a swim after hours,
no one shut the door in my face.
Of course, so many people
dislike the dark. It keeps the same
hours as the recently divorced.

We went to the best motels,
which is like sleeping
in unfinished novels. We slept
soundly inside the teak
and twill, the plaid and brass.
We left the window open
just a crack. It was relaxing.

But this was never our intended
destination. We ate our
continental and packed
for the next leg. You sang.
I read an essay in a journal
that said a real Utopia persists
at a different motel in another America.

DETROIT

America was the real world.
I watched its TV and ate its fries.
We would drive an hour straight
to savour it, the flatlands
along Gratiot, like El Dorado's
dirt floors, drawing breaths
in time with Bernadette, where
automobiles glided on boulevards
paved with ash and automobiles.

The tourist pamphlets never said
that crime was born there, next
to music, but we knew it. Now
we've glimpsed the old police
station papered with mug shots
that hum. And all the pro sports
were played for the same cameras
that filmed a burning tenement.
We would visit it for kicks.

There was always far more money
there, and far less. On paper,
at least, the cylindrical high-rises
heralded rebirth, and the nachos
were better. Coming as we did
from nowhere, it was easy to be
fascinated and still feel superior.
Perhaps I'm being unfair. Our gelid
skins tempered us against the poor.

THERE SURE ARE A LOT OF SIRENS TONIGHT

The little window by the bed is open
so we can hear the ambulances
travelling the avenues like Pac-Man
swallowing the heart attacks
and domestic incidents, the ghosts—
pink and blue, red and orange—
just far enough from our sleep
that it's hard to feign concern.

How can we make it better? Maybe
if children were driving the ambulances,
wild boys and girls, the sort
who chew straw and smoke fat
stogies in the Land of Toys, drunk
on beer and hooting *hee-haw*
through the windows, their small ears
lengthening to equine points.

Rough kids who phooey the cops
and vanish with the advent of colour,
maybe they could crow fiercely enough
to gather all the broken moms and dads
back to their own realm, telling
just enough lies to keep themselves
out of trouble, and just enough jokes
to keep the ghosts from our bed.

LONG PIG

This little piggy went to market.
This little piggy went to work
at the opening bell. With his chip card
and his smart phone, with the blessings
of the cannibals, this little
piggy went viral and put
the dollar sign in "$chweinefleisch"
to get his black belt in Six Sigma.

This little piggy went in a boxcar.
With his ear tag and radio collar,
he went where the work was.
This little piggy got the green light
from the upper cannibals
who wore the clammy faces of his
brothers and sisters, their long blond
eyelashes winking, "Go get 'em!"

This little piggy saw the escalator
eat itself. Racked with debt,
he uploaded his personal data
in order to enjoy a more tailored
mushroom principle. This little piggy
has asked to join your network
and was cured with a magic bullet.
He considers it an honour just to serve.

IDEAL WORKFORCE, FIG. 1

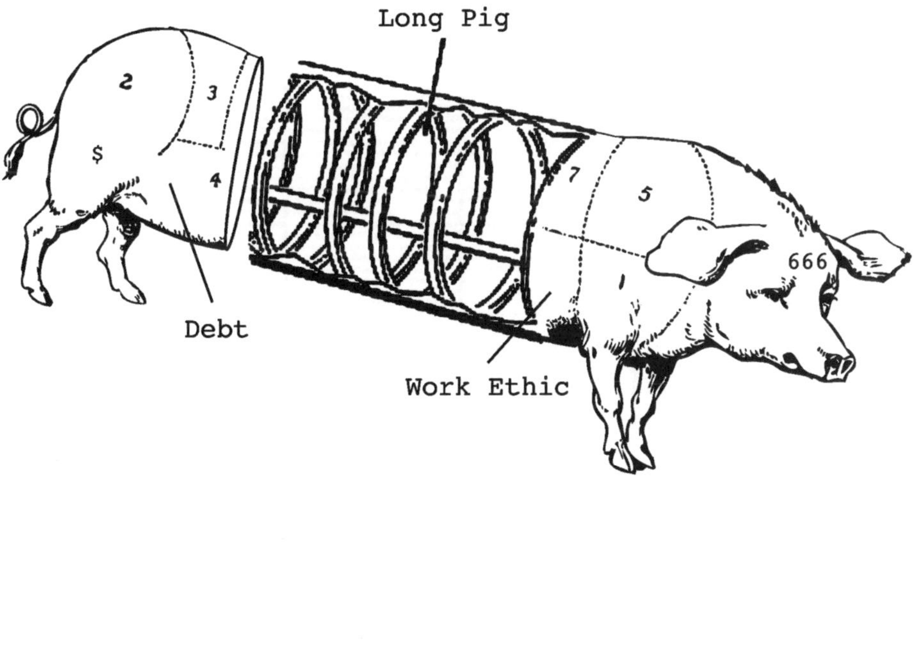

THE WORLD IS SO DIFFICULT TO GIVE UP

after David Ignatow

The world is so difficult to give up so round
    so oceanic and inhabited
the world is where the people
the world is where an estuary once
the world in all its nitrogen-rich
the world that we've come to with everything
    there ever was or will be and it's so hard
    because look
the world where pirates go
the world where rescuers
the world where the lamb wobbly on the grass
    and the man arguing because he's drunk
    and the dark place where the small white
    animal has gone blind and it's going to be
    difficult when
the world of neon signs that used to
the world of flavoured slivers of
the world of exhibitions where
the world gathers
the world of steam heating the deep trenches of
the world of tree forts of cinnamon of symptoms
    and the deep trouble that
the world will be
the world we should give to the swallowtails and
    the flatworms but
the world where just for a little while we saw
the world that sent us to the moon and became
the world where I married you
the world where we learned about

the world getting smaller and expanding and we'll
want to keep it for ourselves and it's going to
kill us when we have to let it go.

EXTINCTION SCHEDULE

For the debut of *Punch and Judy*: the dodo.
For the invention of rodeo: the quagga.
For the completion of the Hoover Dam: the thylacine.
For the formation of the Beatles: the Mexican grizzly.
For the first Soviet McDonald's: the golden toad.

Next, the elephants, caressers of bones,
are slated for the unveiling of a microscopic toy
that can eat our tumours, and the humpbacks
hauled through their migrations, will hang on
till we can travel from Minsk to São Paolo in an hour.

In the next wave, a falsehood will take root,
leading us away from strawberries.
Within a generation, they will take their place
among the sumacs and moonseeds,
and no one will possess their secret knowledge.

And further down the road, the little octopodes
will inhabit crude shelters above the tide line,
aggregate of stones and paste of algae,
and their shapes will form the rudiments
of a future alphabet more beautiful than this one.

THE BIRTHDAY CHAMBER

To mark the passage of time, the child
is taken to the Birthday Chamber—
subterranean walls glazed with small
golden *m*'s. *M* for meat. *M* for mortal.
How well the child knows those words.

How well he knows the hard, sculpted
seats bolted to the tables, and the tables
bolted to thick metal beams embedded
in the cold concrete floor. The archetypes
here are different than in other stories:

the clown, the policeman, the shapeless
humanoid. They are meant to console him
with the notion that the world isn't real.
But the graffiti in the bathroom says,
"The economy is an ambush predator,"

in gold magic marker, and then in black ink,
underneath it, someone has written,
"Dystopias are scary because you see
people struggling, but Utopias are scarier
because you see that they stopped."

6

LEVIATHAN

THE ANIMALS WE IMAGINE

It is not the animals in the wilderness that lure us
to the wilderness, but the animals we imagine.
Still, it is good to be prepared. First, do not try
to be invisible. Invisibility is easy. The challenge
is to be seen. It is the same for us as it is for them.
If we discover that the yeti in the wilderness
is only a bear, then we have discovered nothing.
The yeti we imagine still evades us. Always look
to the future. Do not be deterred. If you think
you saw something, you did. If you think you
know something, you do. You must become
your imaginary self. Now imagine you are powerful;
you are a giant, fiery bear with a star for a heart.
Imagine this is what you are, and then become it.

MY FRIEND CAN IMITATE PRETTY MUCH ANYTHING

after the Flemish of Herman de Coninck

My friend can imitate pretty much anything. Just
yesterday he took a piss like a defeated little
bureaucrat. It sounded just like the rest of his life:
a slow leak. And today he sits down to eat, lights up
a cigar, orders two red wines, and declares:
"The repentance of Nixon!" Then he hides
around a corner. "What are you imitating now?"
I ask. "I am happiness," he says. "You'll never find me."

In the evening, the atmosphere always changes.
The fields stretch out like wide beds, and a mist
spreads over everything. "These days," he says,
"sleep is just something that I imitate." "Also love,"
I say. And we are silent. Later that night, he will imitate
the sound of a car designed for driving to the Moon.

THE MONUMENT

It stands at the centre of an old parkette
by the shore. A man on a horse. A sword.
A sparrow. One hoof steps upon
a serpent curled in agony. A dog of war
attends them, pointing forward.
A parrot with an acorn in its beak
perches on the hero's fist. It overlooks
the port, so that arriving ships would note
the sixteen golden stars, the silver harp,
a glorious marble monument to . . . Well,
there's a mother ferret with her young.
A wreath of grape leaves, too. A coiled
rope. An obelisk. A boar. It stood
for something once. It was important.

LIBERTY WARNING SERIES #3

LASERGNU

REPEAT AFTER ME

I, *Homo sapiens*, accept the Third
Testament shall be engraved on the trunk
of an old felled oak, courtesy of a home
legal will kit. What else is there to say?
Mutter like a cockroach, Scuttlebug.
Creak in the cartilage, the body's
complaints articulating: saying *stay*,
saying *stain*, saying *sting* like a sacrilege,
like iodine, like a good boy. Hey,
Homo sapiens! What have they done
to me? In the ground our bones will drink
the bedrock for a billion years. Can anyone
out there hear me? C'mon. C'mere. Meme me.
Mi-mi-mi-mi-mi-mi-mi-mi! [Repeat].

THE CONSTELLATIONIFICATION EFFECT

We hate to say we told you so, but genes
are clichés. From now on, we'll have to use
a device that can transmit ourselves to a billion
other devices that can transmit us directly
into other people's thoughts. The damn
thing's already obsolete. Still, it works
like a dream—the Constellationification Effect
will convert the human form into a trillion
pings of light that can enter over twenty
billion optic nerves at once. You do the math:
in the future there will be fifteen minutes
when being famous will be easier than
getting pregnant, and new stars will emerge
from superheated giant clouds of gas.

HOW TO PROTECT YOURSELF FROM MONSTERS

Observe the formalities. Call them
by name. *Mister* Bogeyman. *Lord*
of the Flies. Civility disarms them.
Band together. They want you torn—
from the breast, from the page. Burn
candles. Use nightlights. One in each
corner. Let them do nothing in secret.
Look under the bed. Is it you, *El Cucuy*?
Or Slenderman? The act of naming
conjures forth, but it also holds in place.
Call them out: Son of the Dragon, White
Worm, and Troll. Speak each name, but
do not let them write these in your sleep.
Their signature is a row of fangs.

LEVIATHAN

1

She is a sea serpent, a school crush,
a pop star—whatever creature is required.
Can you reel her in with a hook
or cast a rope around her tongue?
The more you try, the more plainly
she eludes you. Where? The airwaves
teem with rumors: Leviathan will not
pull through. Her song of submerged
howler monkeys and guitar feedback
will surface, playing in and out
of commercials for farewell concerts
and pain cream—her song from the abyss,
from the Great Pacific Garbage Patch,
will swell on Music Television: RSVP.

2

Whatever inhabits the deep, she is whatever.
Don't be literal. There are too many risks,
too many depths. Can you thread a cable
through her nostril or pierce her jaw
with a harpoon? The airwaves only speculate.
You awake in your car, already en route.
Dim your lights and drive. Follow the fog
and listen to the same repeating briefs,
the shaking voice repeating: you must believe
that when Leviathan dies, she dies in error.
She does not die to release our secret pain,
or to escape the horrors glimpsed
in chemical light—a light that splits
the deep blue dark from other, deeper monsters.

3

Leviathan performs as needed. Who dares
open the doors of her mouth, ringed about
with fearsome teeth? Her song makes the depths
churn like a boiling cauldron. We don't
understand it, so we think it's beautiful.
When she was married, she left a glistening wake
behind her, and we believed the ocean
had white hair. Now we will believe her death's
an accident, and grieve her as we would
our neighbour in a wreck—a wreck in which
the airwaves still bring rumors of Leviathan:
how her song's gone dark, how the water boils
beneath a bay of dead cod, the many thousands
of her daughters hatching from the salt.

NOTES

"How to Protect Yourself From Monsters" owes its final image to a conversation with Suzanne Buffam.

"The Modern Novel" takes its first line from *The Good Soldier* by Ford Madox Ford.

"The Modernist Canon" is composed of whole-poem anagrams of "The Red Wheelbarrow" by William Carlos Williams, "In a Station of the Metro" by Ezra Pound, and "Anecdote of the Jar" by Wallace Stevens.

"My Friend Can Imitate Pretty Much Everything" is an English-language version (I've taken enough liberties that it would be inaccurate to call it a translation) of Herman de Coninck's poem *"Mijn vriend imiteert ongeveer alles."* An earlier version of mine appeared in *The Exile Book of Poetry in Translation: 20 Canadian Poets Take On the World* edited by Priscila Uppal.

Nu████ Rhymes for Nuclear Children: I began writing these poems in 1995. They have been heavily rewritten, revised, and redacted by mysterious authorities over the years.

"Tinnitus" is a response to Brigit Pegeen Kelly's poem "Song."

"The Vanishing Point" is for Dani Couture, who loves lake freighters more than anyone I know, and also for Gordon Lightfoot, whose lyrics for "The Wreck of the Edmund Fitzgerald" helped inspire it.

"The World Is So Difficult to Give Up" is for Bianca, after David Ignatow's poem "Shadowing the Ground" from which the title line is taken.

ACKNOWLEDGEMENTS

I gratefully acknowledge the financial support of the Canada Council for the Arts and the Ontario Arts Council.

Several of these poems have appeared previously, sometimes in earlier versions or in translation, in the following publications:

50+ Poems for Gordon Lightfoot
The Boneshaker Anthology
Contemporary Verse 2
Cordite Poetry Review (Australia)
Crap Orgasm: A Journal of the Literary Arts
The Fiddlehead
Globe and Mail
Hazlitt
The Literary Review (USA)
NewPoetry.ca
Periódico de Poesía (Mexico)
The Puritan
The /tƐmz/ Review
This Magazine
Vallum
Volta (USA)

"Grendel's Mother" appeared as an illustrated broadside from Junction Books. Thank you to publisher Carleton Wilson.

Thank you to the National Water Centre in Saint John, New Brunswick, for a residency in the summer of 2015 where many of these poems were first conceived.

Thanks to Michael Morse, poetry editor of *The Literary Review*, for valuable insights, and also to Pedro Serrano, editor of *Periódico de Poesía*, and to Helena Moguel Samaniego, who translated three of these poems into Spanish.

I owe so much to my editor—the original misFit, Michael Holmes—who has been a trusted guide for twenty years. And I am grateful to Sarah Dunn, Tania Blokhuis, Jessica Albert, Jack David, David Caron, Amy Smith, Troy Cunningham, and everyone at ECW Press who works wonders behind the scenes.

Thank you to Michel Vrana for a stunning cover design, and to Justice Darragh of Fossil & Bone Photography for a terrific photo shoot.

Special thanks to Mark Mothersbaugh for reading and thinking about these poems before they became a book. Thanks also to Johnny Brewton and Hana Blaquera at Mutato Muzika whose assistance was greatly appreciated.

I am indebted to many friends and colleagues who helped the poems in this book along the way. Thanks in particular to Chris Banks, David James Brock, Suzanne Buffam, Dani Couture, Jeff Latosik, Jacob McArthur Mooney, George Murray, Stuart Ross, Emily Schultz, Daniel Scott Tysdal, and Bianca Spence.

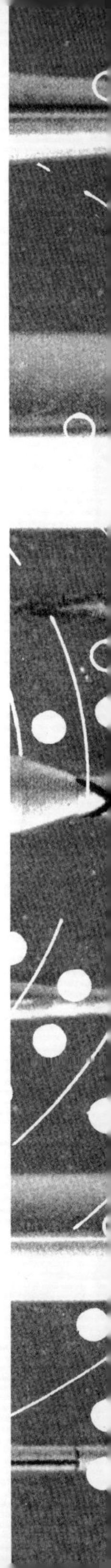